Secure Programming of Web Applications

- Web Application Security for Software Developers and Project Managers -

Motivation: Web Application Attacks

We can read about numerous successful attacks on well-known web applications on a weekly basis. Reason enough to study the background of "Web Application Security" of custom-made / self-developed applications - no matter if these are used only internally or with public access.

This course DOES NOT cover related topics like secure (network) infrastructures, operating system security, patch management, firewall architectures etc. but instead focuses only at the application level - the central field of activity of a software developer.

Web applications are a generic expression for

- Internet applications
- Intranet applications

- Cloud services
- Web portals
- Web services
- Web APIs

Some of these types of applications are not affected by certain attack patterns. For instance, a pure backend for a mobile app usually cannot be attacked through clickjacking - but (No)SQL code injections are extremely relevant.

Typical Attack Patterns

The most common / typical attacks against web applications are:

- [01] Code/Command Injection in general
  - e.g. e-mail, header injection
- [02] (No)SQL Code Injection
- [03] Cross-Site Request Forgery (CSRF)
- [04] Cross-Site Scripting (XSS)
  - i.a. JavaScript, HTML
- [05] Open Redirection
- [06] Remote File Inclusion (RFI) and Local File Inclusion (LFI) resp. Directory/Path Traversal
- [07] Clickjacking
- [08] Session-Hijacking
  - i.a. manipulation of transactions
- [09] Information Disclosure
- [10] Attacks on Weaknesses of the Authentification
  - password handling, hashing, reset, configuration
  - alternative authentication methods / multifactor

Moreover, the application level is related to the following attacks which, however, can only be influenced in a small way by the developer-side:

- [11] Denial of Service
- [12] Middleware
  - exploits, (TLS-) configuration, ...
- [13] Third-Party Software
  - Libraries (client/server)
  - Browser plugins (client-side)

Causes

The causes of successful attacks are (security-)weaknesses within the software. These can be found in the whole application stack:
Meaning the application itself, 3rd-party libraries / frameworks that are being used, middleware, operating system, virtualization stack, hardware, network components, ...

→ Focus in this course on the application level and its interfaces

In general, we speak of "programming errors". However, secure programming is much more complex than pure application programming! Deep technical and interdisciplinary understanding is the foundation of secure software.

Unfortunately, today's applications are highly complex in comparison to applications of 20 years ago. Due to this complexity, secure programming is a huge challenge - even having corresponding expert knowledge! Even 20 years ago, one of the most famous security and cryptography experts of our time, Bruce Schneier, said:

"Complexity is the Worst Enemy of Security"

Hacking Anatomy

First, let's try to understand which basic practices of attacks on web applications exist:

Front-end Attacks

- Requires user-interaction
- Targets active users within the attacking time
- Goals, i.a.:
  - Execution of code on the client
  - Access/Gain/Read-out data
  - Execute transactions with user authorization
- Examples: XSS, Clickjacking

Back-end Attacks

- Targets server systems directly (application server, database etc.) and hence all users resp. the service itself
- Goals, i.a.:
  - Reading a massive amount of data
  - System manipulation
    - to spread malicious code
    - Denial of service
  - By corresponding alteration, all front-end attacks are also possible
- Examples: Remote Code Execution, SQL Code Injection

The basic technical scenario between the three involved entities - the regular user, the web application, the attacker - looks like this:

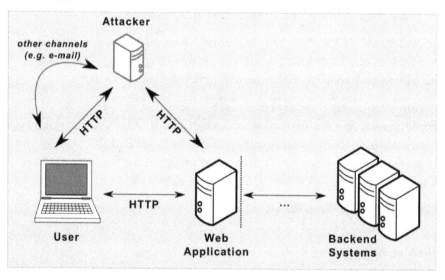

In general, successful attacks which aim directly towards the web application and its backends (e.g., database systems) are the most dangerous attacks. A good example are SQL code injections. However, the severity of the security vulnerability depends very much on the specific application. For instance, we saw so called "XSS worms" in the past: On web portals that let users interact a lot, vulnerabilities within the JavaScript code might be used to spread malicious

JavaScript code snippets. That means, even without a direct attack on backend systems web applications can be damaged on a large scale.

It cannot be classified in general which specific risk comes from a specific attack pattern. This depends solely on the application context. So, a seemingly "not important" attack might be the exact way a hacker uses to achieve a certain goal. Remember that hackers are very good in finding the weakest link!

As shown in the previous figure, an attacker or hacker can basically use three ways to attack:

1. Direct attack attempts towards the web application (direct interaction)
2. Attack attempts through the web application towards its users (e.g., storing some XSS code) or through "rerouting" to a malicious web application
(counterfeit/spoofing, if necessary even including interaction with the right application in the background)
3. Indirect/other channels to the user base (e.g. phishing mail)

These basics are supposed to help better understand the methods and measures of hackers.

Programming Errors and (Web) Application Security

Programming errors concerning the security of web applications can essentially be found in two areas: The input validation and the output encoding.

Flawed Input Validation

A non-complete validation - meaning checking/inspecting, correcting and/or rejecting - of transferred input data is the most-common source of trouble of security holes in applications:

- Obvious user input: Web forms (HTTP-GET, HTTP-POST)
- Application parameters can also be manipulated: Hidden form fields, URL parameters, cookies, …
- File uploads
- HTTP header
- Other input methods are possible, e.g.: APIs, JSON, XML, …

Flawed Output Encoding

Encoding of data must always consider the output context! The encoding not being suitable for data and/or context within the web application's output is also a very common source of security holes in applications:

- It is essential to have a clear definition of application scopes: Dynamic content within the output has to be encoded corresponding to the individual context
  - Context can be, e.g.: HTML, JavaScript, CSS, JSON, XML, ...
  - The important control or functional characters corresponding to the context have to be considered and encoded (for instance: < > " ' ; etc.)
- Less obvious areas have to be included into the consideration, attention when putting data into e.g.: HTTP headers, cookies, AJAX, etc.

Generic Security Functions

Secure Programming:

Aside from the well-known, named attack patterns, attacks towards the application logic itself are of greatest importance.

That means that aside from classical secure programming techniques - e.g., to defend against cross-site scripting, the application logic has to be challenged regarding individual security measures (like permission to perform a transaction).

- Highly context-sensitive, depending on the individual functionality
- Security functions and features have to be defined individually

General rules of thumb that can be applied:

1. All sessions and transactions have to be linked to a successful authentication! Examples:
   - Strict segregation of data from different users within programming objects (multi-threading, session data)
   - Strict linking of every action to the user session (e.g. file downloads)
   - ...

2. Checking and validating all data, value ranges, files etc.! Examples:
   - Numbers
     - have to be numbers!
     - min./max. values to be verified
     - overflow/underflow to be checked – including results of calculations!
   - Character sequences or strings: Lengths, valid characters, special/control characters, ...
     → As far as possible context-sensitive checks (e.g., regular expression for e-mail addresses, phone numbers etc.)
   - Files: sizes, file types (content, not just file extensions), uploads/downloads only by authorized users
3. As far as possible only use filters based on whitelisting, do not use blacklisting!

Well-known Attacks and Defenses

... through secure programming patterns for web applications

[01] Code/Command Injection

Description

Certain script languages allow the "conversion" of strings into commands during runtime. Moreover, in certain situations interfaces between programming languages and (operating) system commands need to be created to be able to perform required certain actions. In these cases, often, strings coming from the programming language are passed to the command level.

Potential security risks are created when these strings contain data from user inputs.

Affected are: almost all script languages (e.g., PHP, Perl), shell commands and shell scripts, but also (bytecode) compiler languages like Java. Java includes the "Runtime" class and hence an interface to the operating system to forward commands and start processes. Such programming constructs can be found in many languages in similar form.

Simplified Code Sample including Security Vulnerability:

```
// (PHP)

//

$localvariable = ' ';

$param = $_GET['param'];

eval('$localvariable = ' . $param . ';');
```

→ Explanation: The code enables an attacker to transmit, e.g., the string "99; system('/bin/echo xxx > /var/log/yyy')" within an HTTP parameter and then execute this at system level.

Secure Programming:

As far as possible it should be avoided to include user inputs within own commands.

If it is necessary to build commands with user-depending data, these inputs have to filtered using whitelisting.

Whitelisting means that a certain list of characters is explicitly created which is necessary for the application context and is assessed as being secure (no functional characters etc.). No other characters than these predefined ones are accepted within user data. Otherwise, user inputs are discarded (or if necessary adjusted). This way - in contrast to blacklisting - not all "dangerous" characters that you can think of have to be classified and collected - which is always error-prone. Only the explicitly necessary and valid characters are defined.

[02] (No)SQL Code Injection

Description

Users provide input data to a web application. This data is processed at the backend within SQL statements or NoSQL queries. A famous example would be a search function, but in general all user data is relevant here – it could also be a

username or password (compare database queries for authentification).
When this user data is processed unfiltered as string within a statement, attackers
could be able to alter the statement code itself and execute this at the backend. This
might lead not only to unintentional data exposure but also to unintentional data or
database modifications.

Simplified Code Sample including Security Vulnerability:

```java
// (Java)
//
// Transfer of user input through framework /
//         servlet / JSP /CGI
// ...
// Building database connection
// ...
Statement stm = con.createStatement();
stm.executeUpdate("UPDATE Table_User SET Password='"
    + strInpPasswordNew + "' WHERE (Name='"
    + strInpUsername + "') AND (Password='"
    + strInpPasswordOld + "');");
```

→ Explanation: For instance, an input string like "Password123';--" (without
quotation marks) causes overwriting all passwords in the table, because in SQL
(not true for all DB systems) "--" starts a code comment so that the rest of the
statement is simply ignored.

Secure Programming:

A strict separation of database commands and user inputs has to be implemented.
For this purpose, well-established programming constructs have to be used. Own
"filter methods" should never be used.

Example:

```
// (Java)
//
PreparedStatement pstm = con.prepareStatement( "UPDATE
    Table_User SET Password=? WHERE (Name=?) AND
    (Password=?);");
pstm.setString(1, strInpPasswordNew);
pstm.setString(2, strInpUsername);
pstm.setString(3, strInpPasswordOld);
pstm.executeUpdate();
```

→ In this example so called Prepared Statements have been used:

- System-inherent separation of SQL commands and user inputs
- Independent of the database system
  → Alternative: "Stored Procedures" on the database system level!
- Included in all popular languages and systems, e.g.: Java, Perl, Microsoft ADO.NET, ...
- Similar procedures/APIs in NoSQL systems (less standardized)

The API documentation of each programming environment contains further details about the corresponding application.

[03] Cross-Site Request Forgery (CSRF)

Description

Browsers allow the definition of HTML forms that address other destinations than the current URL or domain. This can be utilized by malicious web sites to trick users and trigger actions on other pages where they might be logged in (CSRF).

This scenario does not include actions which solely query or read data because an attacker cannot gain information this way. Affected are all actions that trigger data modifications or status changes.

Example including Security Vulnerability:

A simplified example of a CSRF attack would be a web application that enables users to perform money transfer among each other. Such a transfer shall be performed using this HTTP-GET request:

```
https://example.com/action/transfer?
        value=150&destID=33665258971365
```

Since this request only needs the user to be logged in but does not contain additional security measures, an arbitrary web site can trigger this event/request when the user interacts with it. The attacker can perform any creative way to mislead the user to trigger the malicious request. For instance, the attacker could simply use an HTML image tag which means that the simple visit of the malicious web site triggers the event:

```
<img
src="https://example.com/action/transfer?value=150&dest
ID=365884666885" />
```

When calling the malicious page, the browser automatically uses the current session ID for "example.com" and the corresponding transaction is executed. "365884666885" shall be the "account number" of the attacker.
Of course, no image is displayed (the browser might show an error space) but the only goal - to trigger the event - has already happened, because it is a simple HTTP-GET request.

Secure Programming:

1)

Important transactions (especially data/status alterations) must not be executable through HTTP-GET.

2)

To secure HTTP-POST based web forms against CSRF they need to be "one time forms". The most common technique to realize this are CSRF tokens which are placed in hidden form fields (text field using attribute "hidden") and are validated on the server-side along with the form reception. Alternatively, for JavaScript or

AJAX based requests corresponding parameters are defined in code or set as HTTP header to be processed in the server application.

Some programming frameworks or middlewares (e.g., Apache) offer configurable CSRF tokens. However, these might be problematic for certain custom-made application scenarios, but are worth a look.

CSRF tokens must have the following features:

- Random character string with adequate length (or Base64 encoded binary random number - like a session ID)
- Non-predictable (wrong: simple combination of username and counter)
- Has to be refreshed at least corresponding to every new user session or better: each individual form gets its own token
- Every request processing has to verify the currently valid CSRF token

In a simple way, one can think about a CSRF token as a TAN (transaction authentication number) that is bounded to the current user session at the server-side. It will be transmitted together with web forms or JavaScripts to the respective user when s/he visits the own web site. This way, only the requests can be executed successfully that originate from the own web application. Other requests are dismissed.

Similar to TANs used in online banking, their are two ways to use CSRF tokens. Using an individual new token per transaction (here: web form) which means a high degree of security. Alternatively, a single session token is used that is valid for a whole session - but invalidated as soon as the session is. Depending on the application, the desired level of security has to be found correspondingly.

A session token must not be the session ID!

[04] Cross-Site Scripting (XSS)

Description

Cross-site scripting (XSS) is one of the most common security vulnerabilities in web applications. It is often underestimated but can cause a lot of damage and especially follow-up attacks (e.g., session-hijacking). The root cause for XSS holes is completely missing or incomplete output encoding (correspondingly for HTML, JavaScript, ...). A false assumption about the source data which the web application uses to create its output can also sometimes be traced back to wrong input validation and filtering.

In case of insufficient output encoding the attacker is able to add own code into the web application that is executed at the user-side. This can be pure HTML commands or JavaScript code. In this case, the attacker gains full access within the user's current context within the web application.

To be able to execute this (malicious) code, the attacker must trick its victim to call manipulated URLs. This is possible through direct channels (e.g., embedding the code in shared areas of the application) or other channels like third-party pages or phishing mails (compare chapter "Hacking Anatomy"). The following types of cross-site scripting exist:

1. Persistent: The attacker is able to store own code - despite input filters and output encoding - within the web application. An example would be a guest book function whose entries are visible to all site visitors. Of course, in this case also users that are not logged in are affected by a successful attack. For instance: The attacker might able to store this code
   ```
   <script>alert('XSS')</script>
   ```
   under a certain URL, e.g.,
   ```
   https://example.com/guestbook?entry=99123
   ```
   Each visit of this web page entry from within the application/site or clicking the link from somewhere else leads to the execution of the attacker's malicious code.

2. Reflected: The web application puts the content of URL parameters directly into its HTML output. The attacker is able to add own code this way - despite input filters and output encoding. A typical example are search functions. For instance, the following search parameter could be vulnerable:
   ```
   https://example.com/search?query=search+term
   ```
   The attack code
   ```
   <script>alert('XSS')</script>
   ```
   embedded into the URL would look like this:
   ```
   https://example.com/search?query=%3Cscript%3Ealer
   t(%27XSS%27)%3C/script%3E
   ```
   When calling the link, which simply points to the web application the user is familiar with, the malicious code is executed.

3. DOM-based: The DOM-based type works very similar like the type "reflected". However, in this case the vulnerable URL parameter is not included by the web application on the server-side but on the client-side - for instance through JavaScript. Again, the same manipulated URL is created by an attacker. The flawed code is delivered by the web application (JavaScript) but the execution takes places on the client.

Secure Programming:

Preventing XSS vulnerabilities is simple and basic: Encoding of all functional characters within the respective application context - mostly HTML and JavaScript (but also XML, JSON and - if used - plugins). Many development environments include (external) libraries to perform the adequate encoding, because it is such a common problem. However, it is the developer's responsibility to apply it to all parameters of the application. The encoding has to be realized following these rules:

Essential is the clear - at best central - coverage of all code segments which process user data

→ The best encoding is useless when it is not applied to all relevant parts of the application!

The most important encoding rules to convert characters of user inputs:

- & to &
- " to "
- < to <
- > to >
- ' to '

[05] Open Redirection

Description

Web applications often include a redirecting feature for triggering HTTP redirects. This can be helpful, e.g., to return to the own web shop after completing a payment through an external payment provider. If the redirect is not restricted to intended use, it can be exploited by attackers.

Example including Security Vulnerability:

Vulnerable redirect URLs often look similar to this:

```
https://example.com/action/redirect?value=/newpage.html
```

or worse like

```
https://example.com/action/redirect?value=https://examp
le.com/newpage.html
```

If the processing of the parameter which includes the redirect destination is vulnerable, an attacker is able to implant a malicious page as destination:

```
https://example.com/action/redirect?value=https://xxx.c
om/newpage.html
```

Links of this nature look harmless because they are coming from a genuine web application.

By forwarding users to malicious sites this way, an attacker can achieve almost anything. Aside from redirecting users to pages that simply trigger browser exploits, for instance a forgery of the original destination is possible to gain access to user data etc.

To foist malicious links to legit users of the original web application, the attacker could use central, public forums or tertiary channels like phishing e-mails (compare chapter "Hacking Anatomy").

Secure Programming:

Redirects have to be static as far as possible.

Especially, no user-based, changeable input data must be used for creating redirects.

1) Local Redirects

A local redirect is a forwarding to a resource within the own URL.

a)

The best way would be not needing a parameter at all which looks like this:

```
https://example.com/action/redirectContextXY
```

b)

Another way is to use tabularized, dedicated redirection destinations. That means, the redirection is set on the server-side through the parameter, the destination list is fix and read from, e.g., a database:

```
Table "REDIRECT"

ID   DEST

----------------

200  success.html

210  error.html

220  cancel.html
```

The corresponding URL could, for instance, look like this:

```
https://example.com/action/redirect?id=210
```

c)

In case static programming is not possible but rather an open parameter has to be used, whitelist filtering has to be applied to make sure that

- only valid, local paths are used
- no functional characters (e.g., header injection) are included in the parameter

2) External Redirects

If the web application is supposed to implement external redirects - forwarding its users to other domains - this has to be done using static programming (compare to 1b) or whitelisting! The list of URLs that will be redirected to has to be explicitly defined and approved.

An open interface which attackers can use to include their own domains must not be used.

[06] Remote File Inclusion (RFI) and Local File Inclusion (LFI) resp. Directory/Path Traversal

Description

In case a web applications loads files at runtime (e.g., reading local files or files through HTTP access) in an insecure way, the file location address can be manipulated so that internal, restricted files might be accessible or even external scripts might be executed.

In combination with a vulnerable file upload mechanism, an attacker might alter the web application completely or distribute malware to legit users.

The destination of such an attack usually is the server or web application directly (for instance to access accounts, passwords or server configurations etc.). In case of manipulation of scripts or the application's links using malicious external links of the attacker, the users can also be affected directly.

Example including Security Vulnerability:

A typical attempt to escape from a preset file path would use local file system command characters, e.g.

```
https://example.com/action/show?value=/etc/passwd OR
https://example.com/action/show?value=../../../../passwd
```

Also control characters like the null byte (%00) can be used to manipulate paths and for instance end processing paths prematurely.

Vulnerable script invocations on the other hand typically look like this:

```
https://example.com/execute?script=add.php
```

In this case, an attacker would try - also using path manipulation - if other executable scripts (think of, e.g., common web shop systems, LAMP stacks etc.) can be found or even worse, an own remote script might be executed (HTTP).

Secure Programming:

1)

External files and script have to be linked only statically.

As far as possible, linking to or forwarding files has to be implemented internally and must not be based on URL-based parametrization. This can be done by, e.g., using a configuration file or database table. The selection of scripts which can be executed within a web application has to be limited to a fixed list. In case scripts need to be loaded from external resources, explicitly defined whitelists have to be used (compare chapter "Open Redirection").

2)

Using file accesses, for instance including user-based file uploads, requires filters which prevent "escaping" from the destination directory. This does not apply if the files are uploaded to a database.

Storing files in a database system is preferred!

In case of local file access, to prevent escaping every programming environment includes functions to "canonize" paths. Canonized path can easily be used to verify and compare different path securely. Checkout the following method as an example:

```
//Java

class java.io.File

    getCanonicalFile(): Returns the canonical form of

                        this abstract pathname.
```

This method is more secure than building custom filters for file system command characters. However, in case of custom built filters blacklisting must not be used (like filtering control characters as the null byte or line break characters). Instead whitelisting must be implemented. This means, only a list of restricted characters are to be allowed in file names. The list has to be explicitly defined. Other characters simply have to be removed and a new file name created. A special emphasis has to be applied for null byte processing within strings in any case.

[07] Clickjacking

Description

Using the HTML element "iframe" arbitrary web sites or URLs can be integrated into the own web site. This is the standard behavior of web browsers. The "sameorigin policy" indeed prevents by default that, e.g., a JavaScript of the embedding site accesses the content of a third-party page. However, the web page in the iframe works exactly like it would be opened in an own browser window or tab. That means all cookies and hence open sessions are active - simply within the iframe but on a different web site.

This can be exploited by malicious pages to mislead and trick regular users to execute certain actions or transactions undetected.

This concerns especially web forms, functions and JavaScript triggers of web applications that perform data modification and transactions. Simple data queries are not affected.

Eventually, a successful attack in this case works based on "UI tricks". However, there are no limits for the attacker's creativity to do so. For instance, the content of an iframe can be positioned at a certain position, the iframe can be created without scrollbars with a certain size. This could result in just a visible button of the victim's page - embedded in the external / attacker's site.
Another possibility is using transparent UI elements to create unsuspicious graphics to click on but actually perform unwanted clicks on the victim's page.

Secure Programming:

There basically exist two solutions. It has to be noticed that in certain application scenarios it is indeed desired that a web application can be used within an iframe. However, in such cases the whitelisting philosophy has to be implemented as far as possible. That means that all domains which are allowed to use the web application within an iframe have to be explicitly defined.

1)

The HTTP header

```
X-FRAME-OPTIONS
```

is a browser directive which is supported by all modern browsers and restricts the default behavior - namely allowing embedding the own page everywhere. It supports the value "DENY" which forbids the embedding into iframes completely and the value "SAMEORIGIN" which allows the embedding solely into the own page / domain / URL.

"SAMEORIGIN" can be used, e.g., if a login form is made available under a certain URL and included in several sub areas of a web site using iframes. Correspondingly, there might be similar individual application scenarios.

2)

A JavaScript-based solution which allows for more flexibility. However, it requires JavaScript to be enabled on the client-side. In this case, the following generally available JavaScript variable is used:

```
top.location
```

With this, arbitrary verification functions can be built to check the URL(s) of the embedding site (including the iframe) for validity. If this way an unauthorized embedding is detected, multiple reactions are possible. For instance, a simple error page could be displayed instead of the intended content or the top location could be changed so that the own web application will be display - maybe with a warning included. At all events, the actual functionality will be limited accordingly.

[08] Session-Hijacking

This section is about the programmatic safety of sessions of web applications - so the developer's point of view. A secure middleware configuration (like SSL/TLS), which is a basic requirement for this, is not part of this explanation.

Description

The essential goal of the attacker when attempting session-hijacking is copying or taking over a user session at a web application. Here, the authentication data of the users are not part of the attack.

After the successful login into a web application a session is created. That way, all further actions triggered from a certain client computer can be associated with a certain user. The common technology to link a session to a client is the creation and transmission of session IDs.

In practice, using cookies for this purpose is the most used technique which is generally regarded as most secure implementation (of course, in due consideration of corresponding security rules). An alternative would be the transmission as URL parameter (embedded into links or web forms) which has a couple of practical disadvantages and also leaves session data in the browser history.

As simple as the mechanism is - it is also simple for an attacker to hijack a session. Solely obtaining the session ID is all that is required. As a result, the attacker can access all transactions of the regular user - in case no authentication is required once again. This is why applications must not show passwords in cleartext or allow password changes without requiring entering the current password. In those cases, the damage would be even worse since an attacker might gain permanent control - maybe even undetected - over a user account.

Secure Programming:

For the secure implementation of sessions, one differentiates between measures and procedures on the one hand (1) and technical requirements on the other hand (2).

1) Measures/Procedures

1. A decision based on the business context (risk management) has to be made if sessions/cookies will not expire (permanent) or just be temporary. Then, session IDs and cookies have to be managed correspondingly.
   → Here, it has to be taken into account in which technical context the web application is used. For instance, an intranet application which is used in a shared computer environment should always remove all cookies when the browser is closed for security reasons (temporary cookies).

2. In case of long-term sessions, a re-authentification (at least entering password) is required for critical transactions to execute.

3. As soon as a session expires, session IDs and cookies have to be invalidated at the server- and the client-side.

4. The regular user has to have the option to log out and hence terminate a session at any time.

5. It has a positive impact on security if open sessions of users are displayed to them. Additionally, a function which enables users to terminate these other open sessions is very valuable.
   → In certain application scenarios it might be meaningful to allow only one session per account. This implicates a log out at every new login.

6. Linking client IP addresses and session IDs might be an additional security measure but is not mandatory. In some contexts this might even cause problems - for instance if mobile devices are used or scheduled IP address changes take place.

2) Technical Requirements

Session IDs have to meet the following requirements:

1. The session ID must have a minimum length of 120 bit
2. Session IDs should be stored in cookies
3. Session IDs have to be newly created for each login

When cookies are used to store session IDs, the following requirements apply:

1. The cookie flag "secure" must be set
   → Guarantees solely encrypted transmission
2. The cookie flag "httponly" must be set
   → Guarantees no access through JavaScript (e.g., in case of possible XSS vulnerabilities)
3. The cookie flag "path" must be set as restrictive as possible
   → In case multiple applications are on the same host but in different subdirectories
4. The cookie should be restricted to a single domain (header "Set-Cookie")
   → In case multiple applications are operated within subdomains

[09] Information Disclosure

In IT security, one generally speaks of information disclosure when data is unintentionally disclosed. In the section "Generic Security Functions" it has already been described how an application logic should principally handle user input data. This is therefore not part of this section.

Moreover, it has to be part of every secure operating environment and middleware configuration that no hacker-relevant data is disclosed. This includes for instance versions of web servers (keyword 'banner grabbing') or patch levels of operating systems. This is also not part of this section since the configuration is typically not part of the developer's work.

Description

At the application level information disclosures can be caused by - among other things - the following mistakes:

- Error traces which are outputted to users because they are not caught correctly
- Allegedly hidden clues (application structure, system users, passwords etc.) in hidden form fields or developer comments (JavaScript, HTML, ...)
- Output of passwords etc. in log files
- Storing files in public directories

Secure Programming:

Information disclosure leaks are very environment- and application-specific. The unintentional exposure of error traces might be relatively easy to find because all source code can be checked for correct error handling (even automated - using source code scanners).
Most other cases have to be identified individually.

[10] Attacks against Vulnerabilities of the Authentification

This section only defines basic security requirements of user authentification mechanisms. These must be implemented according to the respective application context and programming environment used.

Description

Secure user authentification is a central issue of applications of all kinds. There exist numerous secure authentification methods today. These differ very much from a technology point of view and regarding usability. Moreover, there is a huge difference between implementing authentification for intranet applications and open web applications (e.g., usage of smartcards, user directories etc.). Hence, in the following only fundamental security measures are defined.

Common methods of authentification are:

- Username and Password
- Certificate-based sign-in (X.509)
  - Soft-token
  - Smartcard
- Token-code
  - OTP-token (one-time password)

- SMS
- App-based (smartphone)
- Other hardware tokens (e.g., flickering, scanners)
- Biometric procedures
- Multifactor Authentification / Authentication

To this day the most common used way of user authentification is username with password. The ideal way is using multifactor, mostly two factors are used in practice.

Secure Programming:

As far as possible, cryptographic sign-in methods should be used. Especially regarding intranet applications often an existing PKI (Public Key Infrastructure) can be utilized. The realization of such a sign-in procedure goes beyond the scope of this course and requires profound knowledge in the area of cryptography and the underlying technical infrastructure.

A simple multifactor sign-in can be realized using a second sign-in path in parallel (e.g., smartphone app, SMS etc.). For this purpose it is essential that all factors that are used are assigned to a specific user and a corresponding registration process exists which takes care of the secure mapping.

A secure registration process always includes a reset function in case of token or factor loss.

When using passwords the following basic rules apply:

1. Forcing sufficient length based on the current security standards (at least 8 digits)
2. Ensure a combination of random characters - a mix of letters (uppercase, lowercase), numbers and special characters
3. Forced, regular password changes have proven counterproductive!
4. A password changing function has to force the input of the old and the new password together
5. Passwords are never sent through e-mail or similar (including no initial passwords)
6. Passwords are never transmitted in plaintext

7. Passwords are never transmitted as HTTP-GET parameter

8. Password reset mechanisms are realized through onetime links with time-limited validity

9. Passwords are never(!) stored in plaintext. In case the application implements the password storing mechanism itself, passwords have to be encrypted using current industry standards (e.g., AES-128 or similar) or hashed (e.g., PBKDF2 using SHA512 and 100,000+ iterations). Hashing is preferred.

10.   Strings which contain passwords or fragments have to be overwritten or invalidated as soon as possible

11.   To make dictionary and other brute-force attacks very hard, a user account has to be locked temporarily after a certain amount of failed login attempts (e.g., for 5min after 10 failed attempts). This way such attacks can be effectively mitigated.

→ In case of large-scale attacks which can be traced back to a specific IP address or range, alternatively, this address can be blocked temporarily.

[11] Denial of Service

Denial of Service, also called DoS, attacks belong to the best known attack types because if successful, they often result in news messages in public media.

Description

Denial of Service is a generic expression that means a total service outage. In many of those cases, it is not the application-level that is attacked but the infrastructure or middleware.

A classic version of a DoS attack floods (e.g., using hijacked internet computers that are being part of a bot net) a victim system with (meaningless) network requests to create a stress and overload situation which eventually paralyzes the system. Some DoS attacks cannot be prevented because of the massive bandwidth saturation, other attacks exploit vulnerabilities of network protocols or their specific implementations.

Secure Programming:

1)

A serious SQL vulnerability which, e.g., allows for deleting table content, is by definition also a Denial of Service. However, such topics have already been described previously.

The most relevant form of Denial of Service attacks towards the actual web application is based on wrong resource handling. That is a mistake where the application handles its resources (like working memory, temporary open files, open ports to backend systems, database handles etc.) so bad in certain runtime situations that an overload or dead-lock occurs. This is hard to detect and exploit by an attacker from the outside but not impossible.

An example would be the memory management of programming objects which are not used anymore. For instance, if big images are stored in these objects but not released properly, a single user could exploit this by using a script to create a huge amount of requests and hence create an overload situation.

In general, the secure configuration of the middleware also plays a crucial part (e.g., allowed TCP connections, load-balancer, garbage collection) but is out of the scope of the developer's work.

2)

In some cases, attacks can simply be based on flooding by scripting. Which means that an attacker uses scripts to submit a large amount of meaningless data. This might lead to limited usability of the web application. Examples:

- Flooding the comments section of a page (e.g., with spam or other automated texts)
- Creating a large number of fake user accounts or profiles
- Targeted, failed login attempts intended for suspending user accounts (even if just temporarily) - maybe on a large scale
- ...

A very common technique to restrict large scale requests of this kind is using "captchas". There exist a lot of different implementation variants - from hard to read images to simple, changing tasks which shall prevent scripts (e.g., bots) from successful submission. An individual choice for the corresponding application has to be made.

Very often, captchas are recognized as user-unfriendly. It is also possible to implement certain detection mechanisms in the application and activate captchas only temporarily depending on current circumstances. For instance, if the number of requests coming from a single IP address range reach a certain level or a specific user account is a destination of an attack, a captcha might be activated in a certain context only or only temporarily to protect the web application and its users.

[12] Middleware

The middleware is the actual runtime environment of a web application. This can be, e.g., an Apache web server with Perl interpreter, a Java Tomcat application server, an SAP system or a combination etc.

Obviously, a web application can only work securely if its middleware is configured securely as well. For instance, a well-implemented, secure password process within the application is meaningless if user passwords are transmitted in an unencrypted way. To configure SSL and TLS securely, corresponding security requirements have to be applied. These are not part of this document because they are not in the domain of developers.

Furthermore, an established security process including the patch management of the middleware is a fundamental requirement for running a service securely.

[13] Third-Party Software

Every web application is built upon existing frameworks and uses common libraries. When developing a tailor-made application it has to be taken into account that external components might have security vulnerabilities. Hence, a development process should exist which ensures that as soon as such vulnerabilities become known to the public, the corresponding software is upgraded to the newest patch level or at least the security advice of the corresponding manufacturer is paid attention to in a timely manner.

Moreover, it has to be noticed that by using third-party software all rules described in this document also apply. For instance, input and output formats of data which is processed by external components within the own application have to be exactly specified and encoded accordingly.

Concluding Remarks

The technical term "Remote Code Execution" can often be found in information collections of the hacking domain. This is a generic expression which includes all attacks that work on the basis of "implanting" external code into a server application (server-sided) - such as command injection, SQL code injection or persistent XSS. The definitions that can be found on the internet partly differ. All aspects of this term are covered in the different sections of this document using the here chosen terminology.

Summary

- Secure programming is no no-brainer!
- Security vulnerabilities are no careless mistakes of developers!
- On the contrary, web application security consists of highly complex interrelations and requires time and experience!

Tool-based security examinations - in the ideal way integrated into the development environment itself - can improve the security of custom-made software very much and, hence, make their development much easier and more cost-effective.

In the following, we recommend further information sources which enable interested readers to gain more knowledge to several individual aspects of the subject matter.

Further Information Sources

The programming patterns and attacks on web applications described here are most widely standardized. There is a couple of famous international associations which provide deepened information and material. This includes standardized processes for secure software development:

- OWASP™ Foundation,
  https://www.owasp.org
- The Web Application Security Consortium - Threat Classification,
  http://projects.webappsec.org/w/page/13246978/Threat%20Classification
- Open Source Security Testing Methodology Manual (OSSTMM),
  http://www.isecom.org/research/osstmm.html
- Payment Application Data Security Standard (PCI-PA-DSS),
  https://de.pcisecuritystandards.org/minisite/en/pa-dss.php

Legal Notice

www.ingramcontent.com/pod-product-compliance
Lightning Source LLC
Chambersburg PA
CBHW031250050326
40690CB00007B/1036

* 9 7 8 1 6 9 8 5 5 1 3 1 9 *